SURVIVING LOSS

Dawn Murray

Acknowledgements

Special thanks to all the professionals who gave up their time to review the book, Ryan O'Meara, Michael 'Will' Barrow, and Dr Peter Du Toit.

Special thanks also goes to all those who entrusted their much loved pets into my care when I was a pet undertaker and to all the pet carers who chose me to support them during the most vulnerable, sad and difficult times in their lives.

To all my own pets no longer by my side. To my friend Marie for her support. To my family Cameron, Georgia and Hilda, and last but by no means least, to my husband Dave who has helped me throughout my journey offering support, guidance and love.

Praise for Dawn Murray

"Coping with the loss of a pet is an event that takes many people by surprise. Surprise at the level of grief they experience. Surprise that they can't 'just get over it'. Surprise that they may need to take time off work and surprise that other people just don't seem to understand the depth of pain they are feeling. Dawn Murray has some wise words for anyone going through the trauma of pet loss and this is a book that will provide a lot of comfort for people at a time when they will most certainly need it."

- *K9 Magazine* – **Ryan O'Meara & Accomplished Author**

"As a Military Working Dog Handler, I have taken more than my fair share of loyal companions on their final journey. I have also done the same with pet animals. One thing I do know is that it never gets easier. I will often find one of my companions springing into my mind from nowhere. Sometimes happy memories, often sad. I have found Dawns' book both insightful and taken some great tips to help both now and in the future. As one of the quotes states; 'it's your grief and yours alone'. Remember that in all walks of life."

- RAF Flight Lieutenant Michael 'Will' Barrow Author of Buster

What a fantastic little book!!! The loss of a pet and ultimately a companion can be devastating and very traumatic. The book will help those who have suffered a loss understand the process of loss, bereavement and grieving. As Dawn states: 'Loss, bereavement and grief are all part of our journey through life and although we have to face the journey alone, we can and do recover.' This book will definitely help those who have lost a beloved pet understand the journey that they are going to go on, from loss to ultimately acceptance.

- Dr Peter Du Toit

Introduction

We all experience loss at some point during our lives and for many the most painful of all will be the loss of our much loved pets, so if you are grieving for a companion animal I'd like to say that my thoughts are with you and I hope this book will be of some help to you.

I have written this book to reassure you that the emotions you are experiencing are perfectly normal, so rest assured you're not going mad. I hope that by identifying and explaining the complexities of pet bereavement that I can shed some light on the emotional and physical pain that you will experience and help you find ways to adjust to your loss and face the future. As you read through the book you may be able to identify the emotions associated with the grieving process and why these emotions affect you at certain times.

As a child I experienced the pain of losing my much loved guinea pig Silky, I was about six years old and although that was my first experience of pet loss, it wasn't my last. Growing up I had a variety of pets; a dog, guinea pigs, budgies and for that matter any small creature I found in the garden.

I thought as an adult it would be so much easier to cope with pet loss – how wrong I was!

I have first-hand experience of both the physical and emotional pain of losing a pet. Over the years, as an adult I have loved and grieved for over 25 dogs and cats. I loved each one of them very much and shared a deep bond with all of them, but I had an exceptionally close bond with one in particular. At the end of this book I will share some of my own experiences of pet bereavement.

In 2003 I studied to be a bereavement counsellor however my studies were interrupted due to the deaths of my Mum and my rescue greyhound Kaz. Several months later and taking back control of my life, I returned to my studies and I chose a slightly different path this time specialising in pet bereavement, and shortly after, launching my own company The Pet Undertaker. The Pet Undertaker was unrivalled in the UK and hugely successful.

Following an accident in 2012 at a pet crematorium, I sustained lasting damage to my ribs and spine, which meant I had to close the pet undertaker side of my business due to the heavy lifting involved and long hours driving.

I did however continue my work as a pet bereavement counsellor and throughout the years

I have supported hundreds of families and continue to do so at Living with Pet Bereavement. I do hope that you will find comfort from reading this book, knowing that you are not alone and you do not have to grieve alone.

Dawn Murray

Dedicated to all the much loved pets waiting
for us at Rainbow Bridge.

Contents

BEREAVEMENT & GRIEF

The period of time after the death of your pet is called bereavement. The emotions experienced during bereavement is grieving.

Bereavement

'It's your road and yours alone, others may walk it with you, but no one can walk it for you'

There is no right or wrong way to grieve your loss, there is no right or wrong way to cope, nor is there a particular length of time you should take to adjust to your life without your pet.

Loss, bereavement and grief are all part of our journey through life and although we have to face the journey alone, we can and do recover. Grieving is as unique as DNA, no two people will experience or cope with their grief the same way, we are individuals, we have different personalities, different life experiences, different ways to deal with situations and we all have a different relationship with our pets.

When a pet dies we know we will never be the same again, our lives will change, but we can adjust to life without our pets whilst honouring their lives and ensuring they will never be forgotten.

Grieving

'Grief is the price we pay for love'

It is widely accepted that there are 5 main stages of grieving, Denial, Anger, Bargaining, Depression and Acceptance, the model explaining the stages first documented by the late world renowned psychiatrist Elisabeth Kübler-Ross. Not wishing to challenge or disagree with the findings of the immensely talented psychiatrist, or re-invent the wheel, however the model was initially used to describe the stages that someone with a terminal illness goes through as they come to terms with their prognosis, and was subsequently identified as matching the stages of grieving we experience during bereavement. However, I do believe that to have a complete understanding of pet loss we should consider 7 stages – Shock, Denial, Bargaining, Guilt, Anger, Depression and Acceptance. The additional 2 stages that are important in pet loss are Shock and Guilt.

You may experience all stages of grieving and these can repeat over and over throughout your period of bereavement. I will address each stage, but it's important to remember that no two people grieve the same e.g. you may find you are struggling more with guilt or anger or vice versa, you may take longer to gain acceptance than another pet carer did, but you should never compare how you are coping to that of someone else.

You will identify with some emotions and feel that is exactly how you are feeling or there may be emotions only some will experience while grieving.

Grieving is individual, it's unique to you and how you feel, so do not be concerned if you do not experience all emotions associated with grieving – this is your journey, this is your story and it is you that is important, not anyone else at this time.

You may find that the stages of grief repeat, and many have described grieving as 'being on a roller coaster of emotions'.

Whilst grieving you should avoid alcohol and drugs, tempting as they may be, they will not help with the grieving process and can in fact intensify your grieving.

Throughout the 7 stages you will experience not only emotional reactions, but you can experience physical reactions too.

Physical reactions can include –
- Heart rate will fluctuate - beating fast then slow
- Nausea
- Being too hot or too cold
- General feeling of being unwell
- Headaches
- Lowered immune system leaving you susceptible to colds or flu like symptoms

What helps?
- Take some time for yourself
- Although you won't feel like it, eating something light like a sandwich or soup will help
- Take a walk in the fresh air, take deep breaths

- Sit or lie down preferably in a quiet and dark room

Shock

Psychological trauma, or shock, happens on hearing bad news or witnessing an accident or injury. A stressful event can rock us to our foundations and remove our sense of security and control. It is a built in defence mechanism that protects us as we try to make sense of what we have just heard or witnessed. Stress hormones are released – cortisol and adrenaline. Cortisol increases our heart rate and a rush of adrenaline affects memory and can give the feeling of wanting to run away but being unable to, it's our body's natural fight or flight response. Many pet carers experience shock when they are told by the veterinary surgeon that there is no more that can be done for their pet and euthanasia should be considered, or that their pet has died (perhaps suddenly).

Shock generally lasts for a few hours, for some it can last for days, and you may experience the following -

- Fear

- Numbness
- Unable to think straight
- Racing heart
- Fatigued

What helps?
- Give yourself time to calm down
- Take a few deep breaths
- Take a nap if you feel fatigued
- Avoid taking alcohol or drugs
- Avoid making any significant decisions
- Don't drive unless absolutely necessary

Although these symptoms can be frightening, they give us time to process what we are being told or what we have witnessed but generally pass as we start to accept what we have been told and move into the next stage. Those who witness a traumatic event can experience these symptoms for much longer and prolonged shock can lead to PTSD – Post Traumatic Stress Disorder. If you are concerned that emotional shock symptoms are lasting too long speak to your Doctor.

Denial

Denial is another built in coping mechanism to protect ourselves and avoid emotional trauma or anxiety, a way to dismiss negative thinking. We simply refuse to accept what we are told or what we see despite overwhelming evidence. It's not that we do not understand the truth, but it allows us time to process our thoughts whilst avoiding the facts.

Denial can be as straightforward as repeating to yourself that the death (or impending death) cannot be true, to having complete disregard for what you have been told about your pet. It is generally during this period that pet carers tend to seek a second opinion about their pets health especially if they have been told there is no more that can be done for their pet or their pet has a life limiting illness. Of course some pet carers do seek a second opinion and continue with further treatment for their pet regardless of the prognosis or likely outcome.

Symptoms and reactions of Denial include -
- Irrational thoughts
- Despair
- Restlessness

- Disrupted sleep patterns
- Exhaustion
- Irritability
- Feeling you are going mad
- Numbness

What helps?
- Speak to a close friend or family member, someone who will listen and support you without judgement
- Be honest with yourself by not pretending everything is all right
- Don't be afraid to cry, tears heal the soul

Witnessing someone 'in denial' can be frustrating for family and friends, however with patience and understanding the pet owner will generally come to terms with their current or impending situation and will move through this stage.

Bargaining

Bargaining is recognised as a significant stage of grief especially in human loss and it is important to note this stage in order that you can identify if this is something you have experienced. Bargaining can be fleeting or it may be a feeling that you repeat over in your mind several times. It does tend to be a common reaction to grief in children and for them these feelings may be longer lasting. Bargaining can happen pre or post the death of your pet when there is a deep longing to save your pet or be with your pet again. It makes you believe that had you done things differently the outcome would have been different i.e. the death wouldn't occur. Bargaining allows you to hold onto hope, no matter how futile that hope is. Bargaining happens in the mind of the bereaved and many will offer a bargain to their God or whoever they may worship, for example 'If they changed their bad habits, would they save or let their pet live?' Although these feelings are futile, once accepted, many pet carers may lose faith and slip quickly into depression.

Guilt

Guilt is a very powerful emotion associated with pet bereavement. A pet carer can initially feel enormous guilt for making the decision to euthanise their pet and then to proceed with the process. Feelings of guilt can consume their every thought and no matter how well prepared a pet carer may feel they can deal with their loss, feelings of guilt can get out of control. Many focus on the last few minutes of their pets' life and replay every second over and over in their mind, some believe that by allowing their pet to be euthanised that they killed their pet and their pet was aware of that, their pet was afraid, or that their pet will never forgive them. Many feel that they euthanised their pet too early or too late, or may blame themselves for not noticing their pet was getting old or they were unable to recognise that their pet was seriously ill.

The reasons pet carers feel guilty is endless, here are just a few -

- Making the decision to euthanise
- You feel that you could have done more to save your pet
- You feel that you put your pet through too much to try and save them
- You feel you made the decision to euthanise too early or left it too late
- You feel you should never have let the cat out that night

- You feel you should never have let the dog off the lead
- You feel you should have got a second opinion from another Vet

Feelings of guilt can be a way to self-punish, it serves no purpose to torture yourself when it's simply your perception of the decision that is distorted. Although it is perfectly normal to feel guilt and you are allowed to feel guilty, it's important to look at why you feel guilty and address those negative feelings before they take hold and overwhelm you. A pet bereavement counsellor can help to reframe these negative thoughts.

It's helpful to look at your feelings from a different perspective –

- Rather than focus on the fact that you were the one to make the decision to euthanise your pet, focus on the fact that you were the one who saved your pet from suffering, a selfless decision made from love.
- Rather than thinking you didn't do enough, remember that you did

everything you possibly could for your pet.

- Rather than think you made the decision too early, remember that delaying the decision would have caused untold suffering for your pet.
- In life accidents do happen. It's not anyone's fault, accidents are beyond our control and not something we could have prevented.

Anger

Guilt and anger often accompany one another in grief, and like guilt, it's perfectly normal to feel angry. Feelings of anger can be directed inwardly when we blame ourselves for our pet's death, or it can be directed at the vet or anyone who played a part in our pet's life. It can also be directed at those closest to us, or a complete stranger. Unlike other emotions experienced during bereavement and despite being futile, those grieving may find that being in a state of anger somehow makes their loss easier to cope with even if their behaviour is completely out of character. Accepting that anger is a feeling often associated with grief allows you to accept why you feel that way.

Recognising the times, situations and triggers that make you feel angry and dealing with those emotions in a constructive way is advisable and will help get you through those episodes.

Anger can often be easily triggered by the following -

- Stressful situation
- Irritability and agitation
- Frustration
- Sense of life or a situation being unjust
- Lack of patience

What helps?

- Find a way to release those pent up emotions in a safe environment
- Talk through your feelings with a trusted friend, family member or pet bereavement counsellor
- Identify who, what or why you are angry and who your anger is directed at
- Do some vigorous exercise – running, gym workout or swimming

- Go to a quiet area and scream and shout at the top of your voice
- Avoiding alcohol and drugs when you are angry is important

Depression

Depression associated with bereavement generally only lasts for a couple of months unlike someone who has been diagnosed with clinical depression by their Doctor. Depression is the stage of grieving that tends to last the longest, perhaps for several weeks, although this too will pass. However if you find after a couple of months that those feelings are not beginning to dissipate but are in fact getting worse, you should speak to your Doctor. For those who are clinically depressed when their pet died, grieving will compound those feelings and it may take substantially longer to get through this particular stage.

Depression can manifest in many different ways and you may experience several of these emotions and symptoms –

- Crying
- Lethargy
- Hopelessness

- A sense or feeling that there is 'no point in carrying on'
- Sleep disruption – either too much or too little
- Intense sadness
- Isolate yourself from everyone
- Constant thoughts of the deceased
- Thoughts of suicide
- Fixated on the circumstances surrounding the death
- Not wishing to socialise
- Lack of concentration
- Not looking after yourself properly
- You may wish to hide away in isolation and stop seeing friends and family

What helps?
- Be patient with yourself, grieving cannot be rushed, there is no quick fix
- Ensure you are getting enough but not too much sleep
- Eat healthily
- Avoid Alcohol and drugs

- Speak to your Doctor if you feel your symptoms of depression are getting worse
- Cry, accept that we need to feel the pain in order to heal, don't compare yourself to others
- Give yourself a break, be kind to yourself

Acceptance

Acceptance is recognised as the final stage in the cycle of grief but it does not necessarily mean a conclusion or end to your pain, the cycle and pattern of grieving may repeat itself many times especially on anniversaries specific to your pet. Pet carers who find themselves at this stage are often reluctant to move forward and can actively choose to avoid acceptance, believing that by doing so, they will somehow forget their pet and this final stage, can for many, be the hardest. The term acceptance should not be confused with the term closure, coined by the media at the beginning of this century. Many pet carers believe they should be seeking closure at the end of their grieving however that is not acceptance nor is it attainable.

Closure is not something you should strive to reach. Acceptance however is acknowledging your loss and that your life has changed forever. It is also the beginning of your new normal way of life without your pet, and one that allows you to honour your pet and move forward with all the love you shared.

Acceptance is not an event that happens, it does not occur at any specific time, it is something that happens gradually and often you will not notice when or how, but it's a realisation that you have moved forward in the grieving process. This does not mean that you will never experience those intense feelings of grief again. Many pet carers have stated that they felt they had accepted their loss, yet months later found themselves back in the midst of the grieving process. If that happens to you or has happened, try not to worry or think that your grieving will never end.

Follow the advice given later in this book on ways to help yourself through the grieving process and you should find that this repeated period of grief does not last as long as the first time. Remember moving on doesn't mean letting go!

Complicated or Complex Grieving

For most pet carers after a period of bereavement they will adjust to their new life and gradually over time the feelings and symptoms experienced whilst grieving will fade. For some however, this may not be the case, but recognising the symptoms and getting the correct help is vitally important. As with all grieving there is no hard and fast rule as to how long after the death of your pet you should have returned to some sort of new normal life, however, if after 2 months your symptoms are not starting to dissipate, you should be aware that your grief may be more complex and additional help and support is required. An experienced pet bereavement counsellor can very quickly establish if your grief is complex due to your circumstances and in all likelihood the grieving process may take longer for you. In cases like this an experienced counsellor can help, but may also refer you to a Doctor if you have not already consulted with one.

Those most at risk of complex or complicated grief are -

- Those who live alone
- Those with little if any support by way of family or friends
- The elderly
- Those with financial worries
- Those who rely on their pet for assistance
- Those already suffering from clinical depression
- Those who are already going through a difficult time in their life e.g. redundancy, divorce, housing problems
- If you have experienced one death after another in a short period of time

The signs that your grief is complex can include -

- Overwhelming sadness that is getting worse
- Inability to carry out or cope with day to day functions

- Being obsessed with thoughts of your deceased pet
- No longer taking care of yourself; your personal hygiene and appearance
- Staying in self-isolation
- Feelings of intense anger
- Unable to see a future without your pet
- Unable to work due to lack of concentration, or perhaps you have recently lost your job.
- A wish that you had died with your pet
- Thoughts of suicide, planning suicide or a suicide attempt

It may be that the death of your pet was, to coin the phrase 'the straw that broke the camel's back'. In other words, you may have already been suffering in life and your pets' death was one life changing event too much to cope with. It's not uncommon for a pet carer to suggest that they wish they had died with their pet, or life isn't worth living without their pet.

Although not uncommon to feel this way during the grieving process, thoughts of suicide tend to be fleeting without intention. However, if you find that these thoughts are occurring frequently, please speak to your doctor, mental health professional, social worker or if you have safeguarding procedures in place don't be afraid to invoke those procedures.

Anticipatory Grief

Grieving isn't just reserved for after death, grieving can begin prior to the death of a pet. For example, if the vet tells you that your pet is terminally ill or that you should consider euthanasia to prevent or end suffering.

When we talk of grief we are thinking about the past, with anticipatory grief we are thinking about the future. Of course not everyone will grieve on hearing devastating news about their pet, some may choose to believe that where there is life there is hope and that something can be done to save them, or stay focused on positive thoughts believing that if grieving begins they have already given up all hope.

Anticipatory grieving for many tends to be less intense and leaves us feeling somewhat lost or in limbo, it's the beginning of the end. You may not necessarily go through the 7 stages of grief, but you may experience denial and anger. Of course it doesn't mean that those who grieve for their pets before they die will somehow escape the process afterwards, it is just a glimpse of how you may feel after they die. Some pet carers they may feel a sense of relief that their pet is no longer suffering or in pain and that is perfectly normal.

I'm sure you will be able to identify many of the symptoms, behaviours and emotions that we all experience when we are grieving, and you will see that it's perfectly normal to act and feel the way you do, so rest assured you are definitely not going mad!

Period of Adjustment

'Be the things that you loved most about your pet '

We have looked at how grief affects us physically and emotionally during our period of bereavement. Now we will look at the period of adjustment and what that entails. After any loss, we go through a period of adjustment, this period can be overwhelming if you don't know how to begin to adjust and cannot see a light at the end of the tunnel. You may have difficulty in referring to your pet in the past tense and saying the words dead or died, don't worry about this as it is perfectly natural. With any part of the process of grieving the period of adjustment cannot be rushed, thinking too far ahead, even by a day or two, can be too much for our minds to process.

You may also find that as you move through the stages on the emotional roller coaster, you will experience highs and lows. Feeling high one minute and low the next. That's perfectly normal and you should accept these emotions as they ebb and flow. Don't feel guilty if at times you happen to feel happy or enjoy something when you are grieving, accept it for what it is as you may find the next day you feel low again.

Self-Care

When we lose a much loved pet, we have to address three issues – we have to deal initially with the loss, then adjust to our lives without our pet and finally take back control of our lives. For complex grieving additional support may be required.

What can help?
- Establish a routine
- Improve sleep pattern
- Eat properly and healthily
- Exercise everyday even if that is a short walk
- Be kind to yourself
- Avoid alcohol and drugs
- Speak to others who have experienced pet bereavement
- Don't be afraid to ask for additional support

It is fairly basic but sage advice to look after yourself during bereavement. Self-care is so important yet our own physical health and well-being is often the first to be ignored, in turn making life and grieving harder to cope with.

Working to a routine can help with eating, sleeping and exercising. You may have lost your appetite and not wish to eat, however trying to eat something light is better than not even attempting to eat anything.

Emotional stress is draining and makes you feel very tired. Getting the right amount of sleep is important, avoiding alcohol and caffeine, having a pre-bedtime routine helps. Getting out of the house into the fresh air can help, or any type of exercise you are able to do will help too.

Therapies and alternative therapies

Alternative or complementary therapies are widely accepted nowadays and have shown to have a very positive impact on those who are grieving. There are a variety of therapies and choosing the one that suits you is as important as choosing a qualified practitioner to conduct the therapy.

Therapies are known to relieve stress and improve overall immunity, improve mental and physical wellbeing, release tension and encourage relaxation. You may wish to explore the following therapies and decide what one suits you best.

Many symptoms can be managed through techniques such as -

- Grounding
- Relaxation
- Mindfulness
- Breathing exercises

- Crystal Healing
- Art Therapy
- Acupuncture
- Emotional Freedom Technique (EFT)
- NLP Therapies (Neuro Linguistic Programing)
- Meditation
- Reiki
- Aromatherapy
- Massage
- Creative Writing – keep a journal
- Reflexology
- Laughter Yoga

Memorials – keeping our memories alive

'To live on in our hearts is to live forever'

Memorialising your pets shows the deep bond and affection you had with your pet and it is now widely accepted that we will memorialise our pets in some way.

The ways in which to achieve this are endless, there is a huge range of pet memorial products available on the internet.

Whatever you choose to do, it should be personal to you and your pet -

- Create a memory box
- Plant a tree, shrub or rose bush
- Write your pets story in a journal
- Frame your favourite photograph
- Donate to a local rescue or fundraise for an animal rescue

- Get a tattoo of your pet or your pet's name
- Commission a painting
- Create an altar

Their lives were important and honouring the bond you had with them is all part of the recovery and healing process.

You can remember your pet and allow those precious happy memories to return, that is their legacy to you, and something that no one will ever take from you.

The year of firsts

*'Grieve not and speak of me with tears, but
laugh and talk of me as if I were beside you'*

In the first year after your pet dies there will
be days and anniversaries that are yet another
reminder that you no longer have your pet by
your side.

Certain times and days of the year will be
particularly difficult for you, and will re-awaken
your grief.

It may be your pets birthday or 'Gotcha' day
(when a pets actual birthday is unknown),
Christmas & New Year and of course the 1st
anniversary of your loss. Just when you feel you
are coping and adjusting to life without your
pet, along comes an anniversary as a painful
reminder.

It can be a good idea to be prepared for such
events and decide in advance what you will do
that day to remember your pet, it does not

mean you won't be sad but it will mark the day in an honourable way. Of course you may not wish to mark the day in a special way or be reminded in the hope you will avoid painful emotions, that's acceptable too.

If you decide to do something special to mark these anniversaries you can do something as simple as lighting a candle, retrace a favourite walk, donate something to a local pet rescue in memory of your pet or take the opportunity to scatter your pets' ashes.

What to do with your pets belongings

Like grieving, deciding to remove your pets belongings is a very personal act and should be done as and when the time is right for you to do so, but it is also an act that can compound feelings of guilt or betrayal. Your pet may have gathered many personal belongings over its lifetime and it is important not to make any rash decisions when deciding what to do with these items after your pet has died.

For many, their pets' personal belongings are a constant painful reminder and they will remove these items immediately, whilst others take comfort from those items left in situ e.g. water bowl, lead, toys and bed. Grieving pet owners can be indecisive or even erratic in their behaviour during bereavement, therefore any major decisions should be left until you are thinking clearly.

What helps?

- Don't rush your decision
- You may wish to keep your pets' collar or identification tag
- Make a memory box for your pets belongings
- You may wish to donate some of your pets' belongings to a local animal rescue
- Animal rescues are grateful for pet food donations and some may take pet medication

How Others Respond To Our Loss

Now you know and understand more about why you feel the way you do, we will now look at how others are likely to respond.

Pet Bereavement comes under the banner of disenfranchised grief, which means that not everyone will accept or acknowledge grieving due to pet loss.

Think about it this way, 50% of the population don't have a pet or have never had one, therefore only 50% of the population may appreciate or understand the grief you are experiencing. This of course is not to say that just because someone doesn't have a pet or has never had one, that they won't understand or appreciate the grief you are experiencing, this is merely to give a comparison.

This percentage can be reduced even further when you take into account the number of people who have pets but are yet to experience pet bereavement or those who do have pets and have experience of pet bereavement but view death differently and perhaps were not affected to any great degree by their pets' death.

It's not difficult to see why pet bereavement falls into the category of disenfranchised grief and why not everyone is going to understand why we grieve. What it does mean is that pet carers grieving the loss of their pet, not only have to deal with overwhelming emotions, but they may also face an uphill struggle when faced with those who simply don't understand or don't even want to try to understand, leaving the pet carer even more isolated in their grief.

Knowing what to expect or anticipate how others may react and how to cope with negative reactions can help prepare you.

'We should show a little compassion to those who are unable to do the same to us'

Close friends and family are the ones we instinctively turn to for support when we are grieving. However if you remember that no two people grieve the same, your expectations of what another individual can do to support you through your bereavement should remain realistic.

Living Alone

Grieving can be such a lonely time and you can feel very isolated, for those living alone this may compound how you already feel. Talking over your feelings can help you cope with the grieving process, however if you feel that you don't know anyone who would understand or perhaps you don't have anyone in your life that you wish to share your inner most feelings with, that is the time to reach out for external support.

Talking to a pet bereavement counsellor will help; someone who won't judge you but who can relate to your grief.

Couples

Couples are two individuals and those two individuals may work in perfect harmony on a day to day basis simply because they bring different strengths and weaknesses to the relationship. It therefore makes sense that you will approach and cope with loss in your own unique way.

One may have a heightened state of emotions and focus on their grief and the bond they shared with their pet, this is referred to as intuitive grieving, whereas a partner or spouse may grieve differently by having little emotional attachment whilst they regain control of their life, this is referred to as instrumental grieving. Both are correct and acceptable ways to grieve, although this can be frustrating if you feel your partner or spouse is not grieving in the manner in which you believe is the right way.

Couples and families often find themselves arguing, or worse still splitting up, during or after a period of bereavement believing for example that the other one didn't love the pet as much or understand and show you the respect you deserve.

Take time to talk to each other about how you feel, and without judgement allow your partner or spouse to grieve in the way they find best.

Remember, communication + compassion = understanding.

Families

As with the example of couples, within a family unit each individual will grieve differently. If teenagers or children are part of the family, they will deal with and process their grief in a different way to the adults or main care giver of the pet. Once again it is important to talk to each other and show compassion without judgement.

Friends

Friends can be worth their weight in gold when we are grieving – so let them help. They can help you make decisions, listen to your concerns, sit in silence with you or they can be that much needed shoulder to cry on. They can also help with practical day to day duties, like making a meal for you.

It may not necessarily be the friend that you are closest to that can or will support you the most, it's possible that someone else within your circle of friends will be the best person to help. Accept offers of help, but if you don't want anyone around you, including friends and family that's okay too.

Remember not everyone is comfortable supporting someone through bereavement for fear of not knowing the right thing to say or do.

Colleagues in the Work place

I do appreciate that society has changed greatly over the years and more and more people now live alone with their soul companion being their pet. However it is not a legal requirement for a company to allow its employees time off work to grieve over the loss of a pet, as pets are not considered in law to be a dependant.

Nowadays though, employers are recognising the benefits of allowing an employee a day or two off work (usually unpaid) when their pet dies.

Of course not all employers have the luxury of being able to allow you time off especially if there are 5 or less employees in the company.

Where possible arranging time off in advance can be mutually beneficially to both employee and employer. Check your staff handbook to see if the company has a policy to deal with time off work for bereavement, specifically pet bereavement.

Where possible speak to your supervisor or employer explaining that you have arranged (or are arranging) to have your pet euthanised and if possible to factor in some time off. If you feel unable to speak face to face or via the telephone without being overwhelmed with emotion, perhaps you could send an email or write a letter, time permitting.

Returning to work can be a daunting experience when you are grieving the loss of a pet. You may feel anxious, stressed, embarrassed, lack confidence, be easily distracted or fatigued.

It makes sense that an employer gives you a day or two off work to process your thoughts in the early stages. This is not to say you will somehow be over your loss in a day or two, but in the first few hours and days after the death of your pet you may not be very productive at work. It also allows for good employer/employee relations to give you time off.

If you do have to work because you cannot afford the time off or your employer has refused to give you the time off, perhaps you could speak to a trusted colleague, supervisor or manager and explain how you feel and what if any information you would like your other colleagues to know about your loss.

Of course some pet carers welcome the distraction of being at work and may even request to work longer hours as their way to cope with their grief.

Some may want their colleagues to know that they are grieving, whilst some may not want their colleagues to know.

You may find that colleagues you didn't speak to before are very understanding of your situation, while some you speak to on a regular basis may feel embarrassed and not know what to say by way of comfort.

Acquaintances

Those who are acquaintances or those you consider friends but you are not close to, may be unsure of what to say to you. As a result they may avoid you or make an excuse not to speak to you. Try not to take this too personally or take it to heart, they may simply be embarrassed or feel that grieving is too personal a situation to pass comment on, or they may have little or no experience of someone grieving over the loss of a pet and don't want to make your situation worse by saying something wrong or inappropriate.

Strangers

They don't know you or that you are grieving, so yes, they will go on about their lives as normal because for them nothing has changed. You may feel anger towards complete strangers believing it to be disrespectful to you and that of your pet that they are continuing as normal, enjoying life, while your entire world has fallen apart. If you are grieving the loss of your dog, you may feel anger or jealousy towards someone out walking their dog. It can feel unjust and so unfair, but these feelings do pass.

Well-meaning comments

Regardless of the relationship you have with another individual be it spouse, family, friend, colleague or acquaintance, guaranteed someone well-meaning can inadvertently say something that will hurt you and add to the overwhelming emotions you are experiencing.

Let's look at some of the examples of comments people make believing they are helping you. As you will see, perhaps they are trying to hide their own embarrassment or simply because they don't understand, but they are usually said with good intentions and are not intended to offend you. Don't take any of the following comments to heart, understand that the person is trying to help, accept them as well-meaning and don't dwell on them.

'I know how you feel'

No one knows how we truly feel, but some people wrongly assume that we all grieve the same, especially if they have suffered from pet bereavement. They mean well and shows that they can empathise with the loss of a pet

Perhaps they should have said – 'I cannot begin to imagine how you feel.....'

'Be strong'

This implies that to show emotion is wrong. Grieving is an individual experience, you can grieve any way you want.

Perhaps they should have said – 'It's difficult to find strength at times like this'

'You'll get over it'

We do not get over our loss, nor should we try to, we adjust to life without our pet - there is a difference.

Perhaps they should have said – 'A loss like this is not something you ever get over, but we do heal'

'Your pet was a good age'

This can imply that by reaching a certain age we should somehow accept death more easily, but it doesn't lessen your pain.

Perhaps they should have said – 'I hope in the days, weeks and months ahead that you will take comfort in the knowledge that your pet had a happy (and long) life with you'

'Pull yourself together, it was only a dog'

This trivialises your loss and is often said by those who try to shock you out of grief when in fact it shows a total lack of understanding and compassion for your loss. It may only be a dog to them, but to you, your pet was your world.

Perhaps they should have said – 'Dogs give us such unconditional love throughout their lives and leave such a huge void when they are no longer with us. These overwhelming feelings of loss and despair will pass'

'Just get another one'

Often said as a way to divert the conversation away from acknowledging your grief, however this implies that we can somehow fill the void we have by replacing our pets as though they were a commodity. Some pet carers, even in grief, may have already thought about another pet, if only for a brief moment, but to be asked this question can be very hurtful.

Perhaps they should have said – 'I know you probably aren't thinking about another pet right now, but hopefully one day you will be able to give all that love you have to another pet'

'At Least he didn't suffer'

This may seem like a reassuring statement, but once again, will do nothing to ease or lessen the pain. A pet carer may be focusing on their pet's demise, and in their mind, there may have been some degree of suffering e.g. an undiagnosed illness.

Perhaps they should have said – 'Allowing a pet to die with compassion and dignity is the most selfless act a pet carer can ever make, a decision made from love by putting your pet first'

'They are in a better place now'

Even if a pet carer believes in heaven, saying this to them may only compound grief, by confirming that they will never feel or see their pet again in the material world and should be avoided.

Perhaps they should have said – 'I like to believe that our pets are waiting for us at Rainbow Bridge'

'You cannot compare the loss of a pet to that of a human'

Pet carers are not asking or expecting anyone to compare one loss of life with another, regardless of whether that life is animal or human, and this type of uncaring comment only serves to make the pet carer feel even guiltier about their grief. Trying to enforce opinions or beliefs onto a pet carer who is grieving for their pet is fundamentally wrong.

Perhaps they should have said – 'I can appreciate how special your pet was to you, they are part of our family and the pain can be overwhelming when they die'

A lot depends on who makes the comment and the tone in which it is said. Generally speaking people that utter these comments fall into three categories -

1. Well-meaning and uttered as words of comfort and not intended to hurt
2. Unsure of what to say, embarrassed, or have no experience of pet loss
3. Those who just don't understand

Although it's difficult don't take to heart a comment that was made with good intentions.

If though you feel comments like those above were intended to trivialise your grief or belittle you for grieving, just remember that those people will never experience the love of a pet like you did, perhaps they aren't worthy of a pets love and they certainly aren't worthy of a response; ignore and think no more it.

Children grieving

If you have children in your family or are concerned how a child that you know will cope with pet bereavement the following may help, as children suffering from pet bereavement will not necessarily grieve in the same way an adult does.

They may not be adept at expressing their feelings verbally the way an adult can, therefore understanding how a child may react is important in supporting them through their grief.

- Be honest about what happened to their pet
- Don't make up a story or exclude them
- They often understand more, and are more resilient, than they are given credit for
- Euphemisms should not be used e.g. the vet put the dog/cat to sleep
- The loss of a pet is often the first experience that a child has of death

- They may find it difficult to comprehend the life span of a pet in comparison to that of a human
- They can be very inquisitive and ask many questions in relation to their pet's death or the aftercare of their pet
- Keeping a child informed does not mean that they have to be told specific details

The age and development of a child should be taken into consideration as to how they may react and feel about pet bereavement. The following is a guide by age of the child as to how they may respond.

Infants – 2yrs

Infants and very young children are unlikely to understand the death of a pet, but they are very susceptible to any change in their routine, as well as to the emotional state or tension from those around them, especially from their parents. Maintaining a young child's usual routine and giving extra hugs is important at a time of bereavement. They may miss the pet being around, but other than that, they will forget very quickly.

2 -7 years

Generally speaking, children under seven years of age do not understand that death is a permanent state. Children of this age take notice of all animals in their immediate environment, are curious and ask a lot of questions about them. Children of this age are very quick to understand when something is wrong, so being patient with them, and taking the time to explain that a pet is ill or dying, are the first steps in preparing them for the death of a pet.

They will ask questions and may ask the same questions many times over, as they try to work out and comprehend the situation. Allowing a child to be part of what is happening helps to teach them that they are an important part of the family unit.

Children of this age may want to know intricate details of every aspect of the pet's death, however, it is not necessary to give specific details.

7-12 years

By this stage in a child's development they may understand that death is permanent, or will understand when it is explained to them. Like younger children, they may ask several questions about how and why the pet is dying, or has died. Involving them with the aftercare arrangements for the pet will help make them feel that their opinion is respected.

Teenagers

This age group is already going through a confusing time in their lives. With so many changes happening to them physically and mentally, the death of a pet only adds to an already difficult time.

They will be torn between trying to behave as they think an 'adult' should, whilst inwardly they may be suffering greatly.

They will be aware of how they think their peers will react if they show their true emotions, and will often put on an act, as if they are not affected in any way by the loss of their pet.

These combined factors can lead them to be withdrawn and suffer mood swings, as they try to come to terms with their feelings and their loss.

Children of all ages are not always good at expressing their feelings in words, which can lead to them displaying unusual behaviour, or lead to displays of anger and temper tantrums.

They may regress in their behaviour by reverting to comforting ways –

- thumb-sucking
- biting their nails
- may even start to wet the bed

Children will often feel responsible for the death of their pet and need to be reassured that there was nothing they could have done differently.

Remember that children are prone to bargaining at this time and will feel helpless, as well as responsible.

Explaining to children about the work the vet has done to help their pet is important, especially with regard to euthanasia, as a child may misinterpret the actions of the vet, which can leave the child with the wrong impression of what a vet actually does.

You may want to enlist the help of their school teacher or the leader of any social groups they attend, by telling them what has happened, so that they can keep an eye on the child and step in to support them if necessary.

Involving children in the aftercare and memorial arrangements will make them feel that their opinion matters, they are valued, and help them come to terms with their loss.

A welcome distraction for them could be writing a letter or poem to their pet. This can then be placed with the pet, prior to burial or cremation.

Offering to get another pet for a child immediately isn't usually a good idea, as this teaches the child that pets are easily replaced.

Allow the child to heal before suggesting another pet is introduced to the family.

The loss of a pet in later years

Losing a pet when you are older can be more complex than first thought. A pet offers comfort, security and structure to our lives and gives a sense of being needed.

Your pet may be the only 'family' or contact you have with the outside world and your entire life may revolve around your pet.

You may have relied on your pet, not only for companionship and comfort, but also for security, exercise and social contact.

If finances played a part in your decision to euthanise your pet e.g. if you were unable to afford ongoing veterinary care, this can cause additional anxiety and stress, and intensify feelings of guilt.

Being able to get another pet is often out of the question for an elderly person for several reasons –

- unable to care for a pet due to their own health

- they may not be able to cope with a puppy or kitten
- unable to afford due to financial implications
- they may be concerned that their pet will outlive them and have no one to care for it

Perhaps they may wish to consider fostering or adopting an older pet.

Those who are unable to take on a dog or cat, owing to their own health problems, may wish to consider getting a pet that does not require the same degree of physical care, e.g. a budgie, which is generally easier to care for but will also give much needed companionship.

If the pet carer is afraid that they may die before their pet, they may wish to add a clause to their Will, specifying a particular animal charity that will find a good home for their pet, and that has policies in place whereby they will not euthanise a healthy pet no matter what age the pet is.

If it is an enforced separation due to ill health or if the pet carer is placed in a residential care home and cannot take their pet with them, it may be worth checking to see if the care facility allows pets, pets to visit, or if they have 'Therapet' registered pets visiting.

There are also some charities who will be able to assist elderly owners to look after their pets.

What helps?

- Try where possible to keep to a daily routine
- Talk to friends, family or carers about how you feel
- Don't try to hide your feelings
- Don't dwell on the future, live for today
- Eat and sleep well and get a little exercise
- Look into joining some local clubs, the local library will have contact numbers
- When you are ready you may wish to consider fostering a pet
- If you are still reasonably fit and healthy you may wish to volunteer at a local rescue centre

Missing or Stolen Pets

For those pet carers whose pets are missing or stolen you are suffering from an ambiguous loss. The term ambiguous loss was coined by Dr Pauline Boss and it refers to loss that is without resolution or clear understanding.

Lost or Stolen

When the whereabouts or fate of a pet is unknown, perhaps if it has been stolen or is lost, this is deemed to be the most traumatic, stressful and confusing type of loss. Not knowing the fate of a pet, or not knowing if you will ever be reunited with your pet, makes it very difficult for you to gain acceptance of your loss even after many years have passed.

If a pet is lost or stolen, initial practical help is invaluable e.g. to contact local pet search and rescue organisations, distribute information via social media and to the appropriate authorities, and contact the company that your pets ID Chip is registered to, so that they can flag up the details that your pet is missing or stolen. Make posters of your missing pet and distribute.

The pet carer often neglects their own physical and emotional wellbeing as they focus all their time and energy on finding their pet. Pet carers can become hypervigilant, anxious and depressed. If the right emotional support is not given Post Traumatic Stress Disorder can set in.

The pet carer may suffer from the following -

- Anxiety
- Depression
- Confusion
- Insomnia
- Hopelessness
- Irritability
- Racing Thoughts
- Overwhelming Emotion
- Lack of Concentration
- Muscle tension
- Preoccupation with thoughts of their pet
- Relationship difficulties
- PTSD

Finding coping strategies is important for the pet carer in order to help them move forward.

Coping Strategies include -

- Talking with others in the same situation
- Address anxiety or PTSD problems with a qualified counsellor
- Address family any conflict caused as a direct result of the loss
- Find creative outlets to express thoughts, feelings and memories
- Never lose hope
- Develop a tolerance for ambiguity
- Look at ways to cope with significant anniversaries

Enforced separation

There are a number of reasons why a pet carer can be separated from their pet either temporarily or permanently for example -

- Ill health
- Divorce
- Service Dog Retired
- Housing problems

Although your pet is still alive, you may still grieve in a similar manner to those whose pets have died. Depending on the circumstances, there may be other avenues open to you to establish some kind of contact with your pet despite the fact your pet no longer lives with you.

If you are facing separation from your pet, you can get extra support from a pet bereavement counsellor who can work with you to help find a way through your grief and gain acceptance of the situation.

Caring for a surviving pet - Do pets grieve?

There is no easy way for us, as humans, to properly understand what emotions our pets experience at the time of a loss, however there is evidence to suggest that our pets do grieve.

When a pet dies and there is a surviving pet at home, you may be concerned for the emotional wellbeing of your surviving pet and how they are going to cope with their loss.

Like humans, pets show their feelings in a manner of different ways, they may express their feelings by stopping eating and playing or become withdrawn and sleeping more. Possibly the surviving pet is simply adjusting to its new position in the household; or the pet is truly experiencing a loss of its own, perhaps a bit of both. At this time, we must also remember that the surviving pet will be able to sense their owner's sorrow and that in turn will influence their behaviour.

Allow a surviving pet or pets to see the body of their deceased companion helps them cope better. In some cases, this may not always be possible, owing to the nature of the death. Seeing the body of its companion may give the surviving pet some sort of acceptance, or at least some explanation as to what has happened to their companion. For a surviving bonded pet, not to know where its companion has gone must be heart-breaking.

The length of time a surviving pet may grieve will vary from pet to pet. For some, it may be a matter of hours, while for others, the grief could last for a few days or months. If a surviving pet seems depressed or is not eating, be careful not to reinforce or reward negative behaviour.

If your pet is seeking you for comfort that is ok, but be careful not to allow the surviving pet to depend on additional attention over a longer period of time, a DAP (Dog Appeasing Pheromone) diffuser or some Rescue Remedy may help calm the pet.

Keep to the same routine as much as possible for the surviving pet; walks, feeding and bedtime. This will give them a sense of security.

You should however bear in mind that a surviving pet may have a genuine medical condition. If a pet has not eaten for a few days, or if you are in any doubt about your pet's health, then you should seek veterinary advice.

There may also be specific behavioural issues which surface following the loss of a pet; for example: a sole surviving dog, unused to being left by themselves, may develop separation anxiety; or a dog not used to being walked alone may develop fear aggression towards other dogs. If any behavioural issues persist, your veterinary surgeon can refer your pet to a qualified pet behaviourist.

Regardless of the level of grieving a surviving pet goes through, the pet carer should be made aware that there will be, in some cases, significant changes within the household unit. The pet carer will find that the dynamics may change between them and the surviving pet or pets. Similarly, the dynamics between any surviving pets will also change. However, some may not show any outward signs of loss, and some may in fact, enjoy their new found position within the family.

When should I get another Pet?

Many pet carers say that the pain of bereavement was so intense that they will never get another pet. However, within a relatively short period of time, for most, this way of thinking soon changes. It can be within hours or days of your pet dying that you may consider another pet. You may already have thought about another pet, those thoughts bringing in waves of emotional guilt.

It is a personal choice and no one should criticise your right to decide what is best for you.

There are a few aspects you may wish to consider before making the decision -

- Are you emotionally ready to take on another pet?
- Do you remember the work involved in raising a puppy or a kitten?
- Are you trying to fill a void?
- Will you make comparisons between the pet that has died and the new one?

Providing you are emotionally ready to take on the commitment of another pet and that the pet is not a replacement for the one that died, it can in fact, be a wonderful tribute to the deceased pet; the love you have in your heart and gave to the deceased pet will now live on in another pet.

When contemplating another pet, you may look for reassurance that you are doing the right thing, or feel exceptionally guilty that you are somehow disrespecting the memory of the pet that died. It's entirely your decision and the opinion of others doesn't matter, unless of course they will be called on to help with the care and welfare of another pet in which case it should be a joint decision.

To get another pet should be viewed as testament to the love that you have for animals, and can be an emotionally rewarding and positive experience.

When the time is right for you to get another pet remember to check your local rescue centres to see what they have available for adoption. Many local rescue centres are full of pets desperate to find a loving home, and most have a fostering scheme too, which may be an option to consider.

If you are considering purchasing a pup, a good starting point is KC registered breeders. Please be aware of buying from the internet and ensure you see the puppy interacting with its mother. There has been a lot of good work done by Dr Marc Abraham, highlighted in his book 'Lucys Law'. However there still may be some unscrupulous breeders out there looking to make a fast buck.

Additional help and support

There are times during pet bereavement when you may feel that you could do with a little extra help, reassurance or guidance, and that support is available.

Pet bereavement counsellors are readily available nowadays and most will charge a fee, however you may wish to ensure that anyone advertising as a pet bereavement counsellor not only has the right qualifications but also has the relevant experience and that you will be assigned the same counsellor for the duration you require support. Speaking with a different counsellor each time may compound your feelings of despair when you have to keep re-telling your story. An aspect of successful counselling is developing rapport and trust and finding ways to progress through your grief.

If your physical health has been adversely affected or your grief is complex, you can make an appointment with your own Doctor. Your Doctor can refer you for further counselling to help with disturbed sleep patterns, anxiety and depression. Never be afraid to visit your Doctor with these symptoms that is what they are there to help with, you won't be the first patient with these symptoms and you won't be their last.

If you feel suicidal you must get the appropriate help immediately. Above all talk to someone. There are many good charities out there who are only a phone call away. The Samaritans free telephone number is 116 123. Their volunteers are there to help at any time of the day or night.

Poems

Writing poetry when we are grieving can help us understand our sorrow and aid healing. However, if like me, you do not have a flare for writing poetry, you may find comfort in the poems others have written. These are a few of my favourite and have brought me comfort over the years.

The Last Battle

If it should be that I grow frail and weak
And pain should keep me from my sleep,
Then will you do what must be done,
For this - the last battle - can't be won.

You will be sad I understand,
But don't let grief then stay your hand,
For on this day, more than the rest,
Your love and friendship must stand the test.

We have had so many happy years,

You wouldn't want me to suffer so.
When the time comes, please, let me go.

Take me to where to my needs they'll tend,
Only, stay with me till the end
And hold me firm and speak to me
Until my eyes no longer see.

I know in time you will agree
It is a kindness you do to me.
Although my tail its last has waved,
From pain and suffering I have been saved.

Don't grieve that it must be you
Who has to decide this thing to do;
We've been so close - we two - these years,
Don't let your heart hold any tears.
Author unknown.

I Walk With You

I stood by your bed last night,
I came to have a peep.
I could see that you were crying,
you found it hard to sleep.
I whined to you softly

as you brushed away a tear,
"It's me, I haven't left you,
I'm well, I'm fine, I'm here."

I was close to you at breakfast,
I watched you pour the tea,
You were thinking of the many times,
your hands reached down to me.
I was with you at the shops today,
Your arms were getting sore.
I longed to take your parcels,
I wish I could do more.

I was with you at my grave today,
you tend it with such care.
I want to reassure you,
that I'm not lying there.
I walked with you towards the house,
as you fumbled for your key.
I gently put my paw on you,
I smiled and said "it's me."

You looked so very tired, and sank into a chair.
I tried so hard to let you know,
that I was standing there.

It's possible for me, to be so near you everyday.
To say to you with certainty,

"I never went away."
You sat there very quietly,
then smiled, I think you knew ...

And when the time is right for you
to cross the brief divide,
I'll rush across to greet you and we'll stand,
side by side.
I have so many things to show you,
there is so much for you to see.
Be patient, live your journey out,
then come home to be with me.
Author Unknown

A Dogs Legacy

When humans die, they make a will
To leave their homes and all they have
To those they love,
I, too, would make a will if I could write.
To some poor wistful, lonely stray
I leave my happy home.
My dish, my cosy bed, my cushioned chair, my
toy.
The well-loved lap, the gentle stroking hand,
The loving voice.
The place I made in someone's heart.

The love that at last could help me to
A peaceful, painless end,
Held in loving arms.
If I should die, Oh do not say,
"No more a pet I'll have,
To grieve me by its loss"
Seek out some lonely, unloved dog,
And give my place to him.
This is the legacy I leave behind –
Tis all I have to give.
Author unknown

Rainbow Bridge

When an animal dies that has been especially close to someone here, that pet goes to Rainbow Bridge. There are meadows and hills for all of our special friends so they can run and play together. There is plenty of food, water and sunshine, and our friends are warm and comfortable.

All the animals who had been ill and old are restored to health and vigour. Those who were hurt or maimed are made whole and strong again, just as we remember them in our dreams of days and times gone by. The animals are happy and content, except for one small thing; they each miss someone very special to them, who had to be left behind.

They all run and play together, but the day comes when one suddenly stops and looks into the distance. His bright eyes are intent. His eager body quivers. Suddenly he begins to run from the group, flying over the green grass, his legs carrying him faster and faster.

You have been spotted, and when you and your special friend finally meet, you cling together in joyous reunion, never to be parted again. The happy kisses rain upon your face; your hands again caress the beloved head, and you look once more into the trusting eyes of your pet, so long gone from your life but never absent from your heart.

Then you cross Rainbow Bridge together....

Author unknown

Who Counsels the Counsellor?

'No one can truly understand the bond that we form with the pets we love, until they experience the loss of one.'

As I said in the introduction I too have suffered the loss of many pets over my life, including 25 dogs and cats; from Silky my Guinea pig when I was very young, to the most recent in January 2019, my loving and gentle Staffordshire Bull Terrier - Andy.

No two people grieve the same, nor do we grieve in the same way over our own pets. They were unique and individual too, the bond we shared varies, the life experiences we shared with our pet and the circumstances they died are all contributory factors in the grieving process. But one thing I do know is that despite the number of times my heart has been broken, my heartbreak pales into insignificance in comparison to the love they gave me, and it's the love they gave me that has pulled me through my darkest days.

Sadly the majority of my pets died in the past 16 years whilst I was involved in the pet bereavement industry making my journey through the grieving process somewhat challenging, difficult and at times prolonged. Clients over the years have asked me how I cope with pet loss, one or two even suggesting that it must be easy for me given the number of pets I have lost.

No pet loss is easy to deal with and I haven't always coped well, sometimes I came across as being indifferent, and other times I was on the verge of not coming back from the heartbreak I felt.

Some may find parts of my story upsetting to read, it certainly wasn't easy to write, it is about my own losses, but far more importantly how I survived my heartache to go on to help others.

Remembering Zara & Lucky

I will start by going back in time to 1998. I had two wonderful loving cross-breeds called Zara and Lucky. I had them for just over 10 years and for the majority of that time I still lived at home, so my mum helped in their care, but ultimately they were my responsibility.

Late in 1997 Zara developed pancreatitis. As any pet owner whose pet has suffered from this will know, it's a very painful and uncomfortable illness. Although medication and change of diet worked initially for Zara, her health deteriorated dramatically over the months until she was nothing more than skin and bone and her quality of life was slipping away rapidly.

I took her to the vet virtually on a weekly basis but the vet at the time was at a loss as to what would help her other than to suggest I end her suffering. This was the first time that I was totally responsible for making the decision to end my pet's life.

After much soul searching, a couple of days later I telephoned the veterinary surgery and said it was time for me to let Zara go and an appointment was made for that day.

Mustering every ounce of strength and courage I had, I put her lead on and took her to the vet, leaving Lucky behind with my Mum.

What happened at the Vets still haunts me to this day. Zara was euthanised without sedation via an intracardiac injection. I will not go into detail regarding the euthanasia process on this particular occasion, but those in the veterinary profession know that this is not an acceptable method of euthanasia and a vet can be struck off for carrying out such a barbaric process.

That day, sobbing uncontrollably, I left Zara at the vets for cremation. At that time pet crematoriums were in their infancy and virtually unheard of in Scotland.

I felt immense guilt and overwhelming sadness and could not stop the constant thoughts of what I had witnessed going over and over in my mind. Unbeknown to me at the time, this was as far removed from a text book euthanasia as is possible.

I cried buckets in private, but of course I tried to be strong, I didn't want to look foolish or immature in front of others, so I hid the pain and anguish I experienced which was the worst thing I could possibly have done. Besides, I had another pressing issue to deal with; Lucky.

Lucky stood at the window crying for weeks. She cried all day every day and sometimes for long periods during the night. It never crossed my mind at the time that perhaps she was grieving too or even heartbroken; I had taken her lifelong companion out of the house and never brought her home.

Through my own grief I became irritable, due to her constant crying and my own lack of sleep. After a few months the crying ceased and Lucky took herself off to her bed. She stopped eating or interacting with me and her quality of life was slipping away. I took her to the vets on a number of occasions however he was unable to find any medical reason for her behaviour, nor could he offer a positive outcome if her quality of life didn't improve.

7 months after Zara died, Lucky passed away in her sleep. In my ignorance of what happened to both my dogs, I could only take comfort in knowing they would be reunited in death, but to this day I think of them often and how they suffered.

Looking back over my first experience of euthanasia, if there was a way not to do things right, it ticked every box. I vowed that the mistakes made then would never be repeated and they never have with the pets I've had since. I learned through time to forgive myself for what happened to both my dogs, forgiving the vet took a little longer.

The only positive note was the invaluable experience I gained which I would call on in the career I was to embark on 6 years later.

Remembering Kaz

I have always had a passion and love for retired racing Greyhounds after learning how badly most of them are treated in racing kennels, and I have been blessed to have adopted several of these gentle giants over the years. In 2003 I adopted Kaz from the Glasgow Vet School where he had lived for many years donating his blood to help very sick and injured dogs. He also helped the students learn ultrasound, so all in all a real hero.

He was elderly when I adopted him, so I was realistic regarding the length of time I would have him. But whatever time we did have together was going to be filled with wonderful happy times, and for the most part it was.

Not long after I adopted Kaz, my Mum was diagnosed with terminal cancer. I no longer lived with my Mum, but she lived in the house next door, so was still very much a big part of my life.

Kaz and I were with my Mum on the warm July night in 2004 when she passed away in my arms. If you have ever nursed or cared for someone dying from cancer you will appreciate that it's an experience you would not wish on anyone, either as the patient or the carer. My emotional tank had been running on empty for many months as I went through anticipatory grief and then the grieving process started.

Living alone with Kaz, I had no alternative but to keep working as we adjusted to our new life without my Mum. A few nights after my mum died and unable to sleep due to my grief, I took Kaz for a short walk. It was only about 11pm but still past our usual bedtime. Only 100 yards for the safety of our home Kaz was brutally attacked by two dogs off lead.

I rushed him to the Vet, where we discovered that the puncture wounds all over his body were very deep. For an elderly dog that was devastating news. Thankfully Kaz pulled through those crucial 24 hours, but began to have seizures regularly, robbing him of any chance of a reasonable quality of life.

10 days before Christmas 2004 and only 5 short months since my mum died, Kaz was no longer able to walk unassisted so I made the painful decision to have him euthanised.

I contacted the vet and asked them if they could euthanise Kaz at home and they said they could. I had of course gone to a different Veterinary Practice from the one who euthanised Zara and although the senior vet had a rather abrupt manner with his clients he was exceptionally knowledgeable about Greyhounds.

At the pre-arranged time the vet arrived at my home. Filled with dread with what lay ahead based on my previous experience of euthanasia, my nervousness and anxiety increased when I saw that it was the senior vet himself who arrived. The normally abrupt vet however showed Kaz such care, compassion and dignity beyond anything I could imagine, and that same care and compassion was also extended to me.

Kaz passed away very peacefully in less than a minute, in what I would describe as a 'text book' euthanasia procedure.

I saw that vet in a different light that day and since then I have held him in the highest regard for everything he did for Kaz and in turn me. I did have cause to take a dog from a rescue charity to his practice a few months later and was pleased to see he was back to his usual abrupt self despite me singing his praises to everyone I knew.

Given that the euthanasia process had gone without any problems allowing Kaz to die with dignity and peacefully at home with me by my side, I knew in my heart that hopefully I would take comfort from that in the days, weeks and months ahead.

Of course the grief and guilt I felt was enormous, coupled with the fact that I was still trying to take back control of my life after losing my Mum, I felt like I was back at square one in the whole grieving process and was completely overwhelmed with grief. Little did I know that day, but my life was about to change.

By now pet crematoriums were springing up all over the UK so I contacted a local pet crematorium recommended by my vet to arrange a private cremation for Kaz.

The van arrived from the pet crematorium and the world around me went into slow motion as he removed Kaz from my home in the most undignified and appalling manner.

Once again I will spare you the details, but suffice to say I was left with a memory that will haunt me forever. The comfort I had originally taken from making sure Kaz would be treated properly in his aftercare, soon turned to justified anger, and I wondered how much my vet really knew about the pet crematorium he was recommending to his clients.

On Christmas Eve 2004, Kaz's ashes were returned in a horrible cardboard box and inside was nothing more than a cheap tin that housed his ashes. To add insult to injury they delivered the ashes to my elderly neighbour next door, whose daughter had recently died! I paid over £200 for that service in 2004.

Alone in my grief, I spent many hours replaying in my mind, the disgusting way in which Kaz had been treated by the employee from the crematorium and that led me to conjure up all sorts of horrendous images as to how they must have treated Kaz when I wasn't there.

I had so many unanswered questions about the pet bereavement industry, especially pet crematoriums.

It's fairly easy to become stuck in anger when grieving, simply because it's an easier emotion to deal with, than face up to the painful emotions associated with such an overwhelming loss. I had unresolved grief to deal with regarding my Mums death, and now I would be spending Christmas alone without Kaz.

Christmas 2004 is one I will never forget for all the wrong reasons, but I now choose to put it as far back in my mind as possible. I felt completely alone in the world, the house wasn't decorated with a Christmas tree, I had nothing in by way of food to make a Christmas dinner for myself - it was hell on earth.

I felt isolated and helpless in my grief which was allowing the anger inside me to grow. I had no safe outlet to release those anger emotions other than to strike out verbally, usually at complete strangers, over something exceptionally trivial. I didn't like the person I had become in such a short space of time.

At the time I was studying to be a bereavement counsellor so I recognised all the symptoms and behaviours related to my grief. I knew there was only one person who could help me and that was myself.

The events of 2004, however desperately sad for me, also made me realise that when we hit rock bottom in our grief, there is only one way to go and that is back up! I vowed to make things right and help other pet carers who may be suffering the way I was.

As for the pet crematorium that treated Kaz so badly, I decided to follow the advice in an old saying 'don't get mad, get even'. Shortly after completing a Diploma (distinction) in pet bereavement counselling, I had the opportunity to start a new company and I called it the Pet Undertaker, going into direct competition with the pet crematorium who treated Kaz so badly.

Over the years I gained so much experience dealing with grieving families and of course my company afforded those families the knowledge that their pets in my care were treated with the utmost respect and dignity. My experience and knowledge in the pet bereavement world soon led to me becoming a CPD Presenter and I lectured on pet bereavement the length and breadth of the UK.

I guess you are wondering what happened to the pet crematorium who was so disrespectful to Kaz? A couple of years after I started the Pet

Undertaker, and following the success of a BBC documentary about my work, the boss of the crematorium approached me one day in a petrol station to apologise for the way they treated Kaz and congratulate me on the success of my business.

I learned so many lessons about grief pre, during and post the loss of my Mum and Kaz. But those same lessons taught me that no matter how desperately sad we feel, we do get through our grief and we can take those lessons and move forward in a positive way.

Remembering Molly & Presley

A few months after Kaz died I began to realise how true the old saying 'a house is not a home without a dog' really is and it was time to welcome another dog into my life. I decided to adopt the most beautiful cat friendly black Greyhound called Mac. It was important that he was cat friendly because the night Kaz died a cat that lived nearby moved in with me. Its ok, I did ask his owner if I could keep his cat and he happily agreed to let me have him. His name was Denzil and he was a spooky wee cat. His story has been memorialised in a couple of books, one being Denzils Story.

Denzil and Macs relationship blossomed and over a few short months they became inseparable, they had each other, and I had them. I had taken back control of my life again and life was good.

At the time I volunteered for a Greyhound rescue and my job was to arrange the transportation of the dogs from trainers to foster homes, or foster homes to permanent homes. Once a week, half a dozen of my fellow volunteers would chat via an online forum, no Facebook or zoom rooms back then.

One evening whilst chatting to my fellow volunteers on the forum, the Chairman of the charity, Dave, happen to mention that they were looking for someone to foster two male Lurcher puppies and without hesitation I said I would foster them.

The following day I drove from Glasgow to Edinburgh to collect the pups. I may have taken back control of my life emotionally since losing my Mum and Kaz, but little did I know the mayhem and chaos that was just around the corner fostering two Lurcher puppies, nor did I know at the time, that one of those pups was going change my life yet again and become my absolute soul mate of the four legged variety.

I collected the two pups from a vet nurse who worked for Links Vets in Haddington. Apparently the pups had been handed in to the vet practice by council workers who had found them wandering in a rural area. The pups were gorgeous, well they were after a good bath! They both settled in quickly over the coming days, and I bonded very closely with these two exceptionally naughty, but very funny pups - correction, one was exceptionally naughty the other was an angel.

Being a huge Elvis fan, I decided to call the two pups Presley and Aaron (Aaron was Elvis Presley's middle name). I then got a call from the charity to say that they had received another puppy, this time, a female greyhound, and they thought it would be so much easier if all the pups were kept together. Yes, you've got it - the following day a tiny beautiful greyhound puppy called Molly joined the chaos in my house.

Looking after a large greyhound, a cat and three puppies on my own was exceptionally hard work, but puppies are usually snapped up quickly from charities, so I didn't think I would be fostering them for more than a few days. Unless of course the pups in question fall into the category of being 'difficult to rehome' as many black lurchers are! Rescue centres and charities are full of unwanted black sighthounds – or black beauties as I prefer to call them.

A few weeks later, I got a call from the charity to say that they had found a home for my little angel Aaron. We've all heard about the human/animal bond, but little did I expect to have bonded so deeply and as quickly as I did with Aaron.

The following evening as I waved Aaron off to his new home he looked so confused and sad, wondering why I handed him over to strangers - his new family, and as they drove away I literally collapsed to my knees and cried my heart out. My beautiful, sweet angel Aaron was away to begin a new life without me.

His new family changed his name to Robbie, and I was to see him again on two more occasions, once when he was 2yrs old and the second time when he was 10yrs old. I always spoke fondly of my angel Aaron wondering how he was doing in his home and missing him dreadfully.

Although I never left Presley and Molly for more than an hour, safely tucked up together in a huge crate, Presley became a renowned escape artist, and once out of his crate he chewed everything and anything within his reach and with his long lanky legs he could easily jump up on kitchen units giving him access to most of the kitchen appliances.

For his safety while I was out of the house, I purchased a padlock for the crate, so you can imagine my surprise when I returned home to find he had once again escaped and damaged all the new appliances I had just replaced. I then purchased another padlock, one for the top of the crate door and one for the bottom, but even that didn't stop my little Houdini, and he somehow managed to squeeze out through the gap of crate door.

To give you an example of what he damaged, over a period of one week, he chewed his way through the washing machine handle and the rubber seal inside, 3 kettles, 2 toasters, an electric can opener and part of the wall! No one warned me that lurchers are highly intelligent dogs and Presley was by far the smartest pup I had ever known. I literally couldn't turn my back on Presley for one second, otherwise he was chewing his way through something else. He had plenty of his own puppy toys to chew on, but showed little interest in them. His constant and faithful companion Molly was always by his side egging him on, but never participating.

Finally I had to claim on my home insurance. The insurance assessor arrived to value the damage Presley had done, not only inside the house but also in my garden. The cost to replace all the items damaged or chewed was in the region of ten thousand pounds. Yes, you read that right, ten *thousand* pounds. The bombshell was still to come; although I was insured for damage done by Presley, the small print stated that the insurance company would only replace one damaged item per claim. The insurance assessor kindly advised me to claim for a new back door (Presley had chewed that rubber seal too), being the single most expensive item to replace. I had to pay for the rest of the damage myself.

Fostering certainly had its challenges. I knew in my heart that if Presley continued to behave like that once he was adopted in a new home, he would soon find himself back at the rescue, probably time and time again. He certainly made Marley, from the movie Marley & Me, look positively docile in comparison. But I loved the big, goofy, friendly and highly amusing lurcher.

In desperation, I enrolled Presley in dog training classes. If you have ever been to dog training classes you will know that it's never the dogs fault but the owners, and in most cases it's the owners who benefit from being trained! I certainly learned a lot, but Presley excelled in all his obedience training, mastering Target Training within a few weeks, the type of training usually reserved for older more experienced dogs.

Regardless of all his success at obedience training, Presley continued to be a complete nightmare of a puppy, Molly on the other hand, was an absolute delight. One day I asked a friend to help me look after them as I tried to get my house back in order. My friend assured me she would look after Presley and Molly in my enclosed garden and I was not to worry, they would be fine. Knowing what Presley was like, I decided to check on them a couple of minutes later, only to discover Presley had escaped from the garden! He managed to squeeze through the wrought iron gate unseen and wander off down the road. Thankfully he did not get too far before I found him and he did the walk of shame back home.

Finally I got an email from the charity stating that I was to get Presley neutered prior to being adopted, as they had a family in mind who were interested in adopting him. I took him to the vet as instructed. I explained to the vet that they would need to be careful with Presley as he was a bit of a handful. The vet assured me in a rather patronising manner that they had plenty of experience of looking after pups, so you can imagine my amusement when I realised that as she was explaining her vast experience with pups (whilst cuddling Presley), that he had merrily chewed the entire way through her stethoscope!

Four hours later the vet telephoned me to say that his operation had gone well and I could go and collect him. She added, I'm sorry to tell you that we hung Presley's collar, lead and coat over the front of the crate and he chewed his way through them whilst waiting for his op!

With that in mind and taking all the damage to my home into consideration I contacted Dave at the charity. I told him that if Presley and Molly were being adopted by anyone, then that person would be me! I couldn't envisage ever being parted from my funny, lanky, and very naughty lurcher, so I officially adopted Presley and his co-conspirator Molly.

In doing so, I had now joined the ranks of being a failed fosterer. Fostering is such an essential part of any pet rescue, but given the fact I fall in love and bond so quickly with pets, I wasn't cut out to foster. I did attempt to foster again a few years later, and yes, I failed again. Hardly surprising I always had a home full of dogs and cats.

With my hands full looking after my four legged family I gave up volunteering for the charity, however, I kept in touch with Dave who became a very good friend to me and a few years later, I'm delighted to say he also became my husband.

During his time in charge of the greyhound rescue, he successfully rehomed hundreds and hundreds of retired racing Greyhounds. He was one of the most successful rehoming co-ordinators any UK greyhound charity had known.

In February 2006 Mac, Denzil, Presley, Molly and I moved to Lanark to live with Dave, his 3 greyhounds, Ivor, Ruby and Wizard and his cat Six.

We lived happily in the Lanark area for the next ten years, although having that number of pets, as they grew old, sadness and grief were never far away.

Mac and Denzil remained firm friends and when Denzil died Mac withdrew from the company of the other dogs preferring to spend time on his own. Sadly he chose to be a loner until the day he died.

Ivor and Wizard had also died by then, although we had adopted more rescue dogs along the way and gave a home to two unwanted cats. Presley remained the class clown throughout the years with his faithful Molly by his side, making us laugh every day, and by then he had become an international star, shortening his name to KP (King Presley) with his own Facebook account, entertaining his fans with his famous true stories and money saving tips!

In February 2015 we were out in the garden when Molly let out the most horrific ear piercing scream I had ever heard. She tried to walk towards me but was unable to move, so I carried her back to the house and phoned the vet immediately. Living in the Lanark area, we were within driving distance of the Armac Veterinary Practice, Biggar. The senior partner David Gardner-Roberts is the most genuine, compassionate and knowledgeable vet I had ever known and our cats and dogs were always in good hands whilst in his care.

Over the years, not only did we get to know David but also his entire superb team, who all played their part by supporting us and sharing their invaluable knowledge.

I rushed Molly to Armac and waited while they x-rayed her leg. David called me into the consultation room to view Mollys x-rays, but I knew by the look on his face it wasn't good news. The entire length of Mollys hind leg had shattered into a thousand pieces due to a tumour, she must have been in excruciating pain.

We discussed the options available, including amputation, however we agreed that given Molly was now approaching her 10th birthday, invasive surgery and potential chemotherapy was not necessarily in her best interests.

The decision was made to euthanise Molly whilst still sedated. Of course we had Presley with us, as I said previously, the two were never apart and where one went the other one went.

David let us take Presley through to the room where Molly remained heavily sedated. Through our tears, Dave and I said our last goodbyes to Molly, but the most heart-breaking of all was the sadness in Presley's eyes as he gently licked his beloved Molly's nose as his way of saying 'I love you Molly, till we meet again'.

We brought Molly home with us, in preparation for the 5 hour drive to Pet Funeral Services in North Wales for her cremation. Through my work as a pet undertaker I visited many pet crematoriums in the UK and in my opinion the most outstanding is in North Wales. Not only is this cemetery and crematorium the best in the UK, the level of service, dignity and respect they show not only to the pets in their care, but also to pet carers is second to none. The 5 hour drive from our home in Lanark to Holywell in North Wales is a painful but worthwhile drive.

Presley was never the same after Molly died. The sadness remained in his eyes, the same sadness that was evident when Molly was euthanised. He had our other dogs for company and being the sociable dog that he was he was never alone, but he never interacted or bonded with the other dogs to the same extent as he had with Molly. It was heart-breaking to see my boy this way every day and not be able to take away his sadness. Sadly, no longer the class clown, but he remained a mummy's boy throughout, and I comforted him as much as I possibly could.

18 months later Presley developed a limp in his front leg. I had a gut feeling what was wrong, so rather than treat him for arthritis I asked the vets at Armac to x-ray his leg. My worst fears became a reality, when they confirmed that Presley had osteosarcoma (bone cancer), the tumour was on his knee.

For months my courageous boy hid from me the excruciating pain he must have experienced. Despite knowing in my heart what was wrong with him, shock took over and I felt like my heart was being ripped out of my body, I felt physically sick and thought I was going to pass out.

I was devastated beyond words and I felt like my whole world was crashing down around me.

The decision to do what was best for Presley had to be mine and mine alone. It's a heavy burden to carry.

I had so many factors to take into consideration. Yes, there was the option to amputate, but I knew that was not something a big dog like Presley would have been comfortable with. A few years earlier our greyhound Ruby was diagnosed with osteosarcoma and we opted to have her leg amputated with a follow-up course of chemotherapy. Thanks to the wonderful care she received at Edinburgh Veterinary School Ruby managed exceptionally well, and lived for a further four years, but she wasn't Presley and her circumstances were different.

The love I had for Presley was so strong that I couldn't put my boy through the pain and uncertainty just for my own selfish reasons.

I also had to take his age into consideration (he was almost 11). But most importantly I had to consider the fact that he been heartbroken since Molly died.

So, I made my decision, I had to let Presley go, to die with dignity and more importantly to save him suffering. I knew in my heart it was the right thing to do. Dying with dignity, there would be no more pain or sadness for my beloved boy and he would finally be reunited with his beloved Molly.

Presley died peacefully in my arms on Friday 26th August 2016 at Armac Veterinary Surgery, knowing that his mum and dad who loved him so much were with him at the end.

He was cremated at Pet Funeral Services, North Wales, two days later, in a ceremony fit for a King.

I worshipped the ground Presley walked on, but this was one loss I wasn't going to recover from easily and I doubt I will ever fully recover - something I've come to accept. Presley's life will not be remembered in sadness and grief, he will be remembered for all the love and laughter he brought to so many people throughout his life. He would not want me to be sad, and difficult as that has been for me, I will always remember my handsome funny Lurcher who was born a pauper and died a King.

Every room in my home has a framed photo of Presley, he had such a big personality in life and his huge presence lives on to this day. I take comfort in knowing that Presley and Molly are reunited, and of course not forgetting Presley's brother Aaron, who I heard died only a few months after him.

In order for me to carry on with the work that I do, supporting others through pet loss, every time those overwhelming feelings of sadness creep into my mind, I dismiss them and turn my thoughts to happier times. This may sound easy but it's taken me a lot of practice over the years to perfect it. It involves reframing my thoughts. Taking control of my sad and negative emotions allows me to turn them into happy and positive memories. Pet carers are often reminded when grieving the loss of a pet, that the sadness will pass and they will be left with the happy memories. This is something we all strive to achieve, but in my case I need that process to work a little faster in order to support others, hence the reason I also use recognised therapies and techniques to help myself, the same as I do when supporting pet carers through bereavement.

We never truly get over such a profound loss, but we can adapt to a new way of life without our pets. Using recognised therapies can help and if at first you don't think a particular therapy is helping, don't give up, try another therapy, some techniques take practise. Less than two hours after my own dog Basil was euthanised at home, I was standing in a veterinary practice supporting one of my clients as their much loved family dog was euthanised. The vet remarked to me at the time, that it couldn't be easy for me to do the job I do, if only he knew, just how difficult that day actually was for me.

Pet carers often try to impress upon me just how much their pets meant to them, they tell me that their pet was their soul mate and in the hope that I will understand and appreciate the depth of their grieving. Well I do understand, I have suffered the pain too many times and of course the loss of my own four legged soul mate -Presley.

My experience didn't end with the loss of Presley, each one of my pets were loved very much and when each one died I grieved differently, but all were painful. I was with all my pets when they were euthanised, each one a different experience and a different story, but to recount all my stories would be a book in itself.

I have been asked so many times over the years to share my own experiences of pet loss and this was the right time for me to do that. I have so many pet loss scars on my heart from the pain I have lived through. I know these wounds can be opened at any time, but I prefer to keep them closed, to remember my pets with all the love and happiness they gave me and in doing so I honour their lives by keeping their memory alive.

Lucky and Zara

Kaz

Mac and Denzil

Presley (l) and Aaron (r) the day they were
handed in to the vet in Haddington

Molly

My soulmate Presley (KP)

In loving memory of all my pets

My Dogs
Andy, Lily, Maisie, Murphy, Basil, Mutley,
Mandy, Presley, Molly, Mabel, Sweetie, Ruby, Mac,
Wizard, Ivor, Kaz, Lucky, Zara, Randy and Kim.

My Cats
Denzil, Six, Olly, Zorro, Charlie and Stan

My Canaries
Captain and Tennille

And last but not least all the guinea pigs and
budgies I had as a child

All waiting patiently for me at Rainbow Bridge,
till we meet again.

Appendix

I hope that my book has helped you and made a difference as you continue your journey through bereavement. Our pets gave us so much love and it is that same love that help pull us through our darkest days and go forward in life remembering the joy and happiness we shared with them.

Each one so special in their own way, and each one remembered with all the love in the world. Sure, from time to time you will have sad days, and I wish I could save you from that pain, but I hope that all those wonderful memories and the love you received from your pet will help pull you through your darkest days.

I hope you will continue to heal and the intense pain will soon be in the past and you too can move forward with your wonderful memories.

'To live on in our hearts is to live forever'

If my book has helped you in some way and I hope it has, I would really appreciate it if you could leave a review on Amazon. Thank you.

If you need additional support while you are grieving please do not hesitate to contact us at Living with Pet Bereavement, our website is www.livingwithpetbereavement.com

Through the work we do at Living with Pet Bereavement we founded the Ray of Hope Appeal. Over the years we have raised thousands of pounds to help various animal charities and good causes for example, Edinburgh Vet School, Greyhound Rescues, Street Dogs in Beirut, Pet Search & Rescue and many more. If you wish to donate, details can be found on the Living with Pet Bereavement website.

The profits from the sale of this book will be equally divided to help animal charities. The recipients being: National Military Working Dog Memorial, Nowzad and the Ray of Hope Appeal at Living with pet bereavement.

For more information visit their websites –
www.nmwdm.org.uk
www.nowzad.com
www.livingwithpetbereavement.com